ARCHERY

BOY SCOUTS OF AMERICA
IRVING, TEXAS

Requirements

1. Do the following:
   a. Name and explain the archery safety rules.
   b. Tell about the local and state laws on ownership, use, and registration of archery tackle.
2. Do the following:
   a. Name and point out the parts of an arrow.
   b. Name and point out the parts of a bow.
   c. Describe and show how to use an arm guard, shooting glove, finger tab, and quiver.
3. Do the following:
   a. Explain proper care of and how to store the bow, bowstring, arrows, and leather items.
   b. Make a bowstring and use it.
   c. Make one complete arrow from a bare shaft.
   d. Explain the following terms: cast, bow weight, string height (fist-mele), aiming, spine, mechanical release, freestyle, and bare bow.
   e. Describe the different types of arrows.
   f. Show the nine basic steps of a good shooting method.
   g. Locate and mark with dental floss, crimp on, or other method, the nocking point on a bow string.
4. Do ONE of the following:
   a. Shoot with bow and arrows, using a finger release, one round from any one of the following NFAA field rounds and indoor rounds:
      (1) A field round of 14 targets and make a score of 60 points.
      (2) An indoor round and make a score of 50 points.
      (3) A 900 round and make a score of 225 points.*
      (4) An indoor FITA round I and make a score of 80 points.†
                              OR
   b. As a member of a National Archery Association (NAA) Junior Olympic Archery Development Club, qualify as a Yeoman, Junior Bowman, and Bowman.
                              OR
   c. As a member of the NFAA Junior Division, qualify as a Cub or Youth

by earning 100-score Progression Patches.
5. Explain the following:
    a. The difference between field and target archery.
    b. Field round, hunter round, and animal round.
    c. Scout field round.
    d. Indoor field rounds.
    e. 900, Junior 900, Easton, and Junior Easton rounds.
    f. Indoor FITA rounds I and II.
    g. FITA and Junior FITA rounds.
    h. Junior Olympic qualification rounds.
    i. The importance of obedience to a rangemaster or other person in charge of a range.

*Intermediates—15–17 years old
†Juniors—up to 14 years old

Contents

33259
ISBN 0-8395-3259-8
©1986 Boy Scouts of America
2001 Printing of the 1986 Edition

Introduction

The bow and arrow, like speech and the use of fire, has played an important part in the advancement of civilization. Fire provided warmth and some protection from wild animals. Speech enabled man to convey ideas and information. And the bow and arrow gave man a safer and easier way to hunt. Imagine man's excitement when he first discovered that with a "strung stick" he could hunt animals from a safe distance. Fish and game that had been impossible to obtain came within his reach.

The bow and arrow remained a major factor in man's life until long after the development of gunpowder.

Today the bow and arrow are used primarily for sport. Target archery and bow hunting are practiced all over the world. While the principles of archery have not changed since its discovery, the equipment has improved a lot. Bows today are no longer made of a single piece of yew wood. They are made of wood, fiberglass, and metal. These composite bows provide a degree of speed and accuracy that would have amazed longbowmen like Robin Hood and the ancient Turkish, Moorish, Phoenician, and Egyptian archers who came before him.

As an archer you will learn new skills and share in an adventure as old as history. You will learn the joy of shooting an arrow exactly where you want it to go, and you will gain a sport that can last a lifetime. Good luck and good shooting.

Archery Safety Rules

Archery is lots of fun, but the fun can quickly turn into tragedy unless every archer observes some common-sense safety rules.

Before you even think about using your bow, learn these rules and make up your mind to follow them every time you hold a bow. Remember, most accidents are the result of carelessness and thoughtlessness.

As a Scout and an archer, you must learn and practice these few simple rules:

1. Always walk, never run, on the archery range. If you run, you might accidentally cross in front of another archer, step on arrows lying on the ground, or trip and fall into the target and be injured by arrows sticking out of it.

2. Always aim and shoot only at a definite target; never shoot just for the sake of shooting. Always be sure you know what your target is and that it is safe to shoot at. If you are not sure, take a closer look. If, after a closer look, you are still not sure, do not shoot.

3. Always be sure the area around and behind your target is clear before you shoot.

4. Never shoot at a target that is too thin to stop an arrow. Never shoot if there is a chance your arrow may ricochet from the target or another object and hit someone.

5. Always use proper safety equipment, including an arm guard, finger tab, and finger or wrist sling.

6. Always use arrows of the proper length for you. Arrows that are too short can cause serious injuries.

7. Always inspect your equipment before shooting. Damaged equipment should be repaired or replaced to avoid injuries. Replace the bowstring whenever it becomes worn.

8. Always have an arrow on the string when shooting the bow. "Dryfiring," shooting a bow without an arrow, can seriously damage the bow.

9. Always wait to retrieve your arrows until other archers are through shooting; wait until the "all clear" is given.
10. In field archery, when recovering arrows, always lean your bow against the face of the target to warn archers who may be following you that you are behind the target.
11. In target archery, if there are more than four archers, or more than one target in use, a field captain and whistle should be used for overall safety and control. One whistle blast means "start shooting," two mean "cease firing—all clear" (retrieve arrows and score), and four or more blasts mean "cease firing—emergency" (remain at the firing line for further instructions).
12. Never shoot an arrow straight up into the air.

Never walk across the shooting line until the "all clear" is given. Reach with your bow to retrieve a misfired arrow.

Laws on Archery

Many states and local communities have laws governing archers. Some laws cover ownership and registration of archery tackle. Others govern hunting and fishing with bow and arrow.

Ask your merit badge counselor or members of a local archery club about the laws in your area.

Do not stand too close to the target when picking up score sheets.

Archery Equipment

Having the right equipment is as important as having proper instruction on how to shoot. Your equipment should fit you and your shooting requirements. It is to your advantage to find an experienced archer to help you choose the right tackle.

The Bow

A bow may be made of wood, fiberglass, aluminum, steel, or magnesium, and is usually made of a combination of these materials.

You may select a single-piece bow, which does not come apart, or a take-down bow, which breaks into three sections: a handle riser and upper and lower limbs. Take-down bows are easier to store and more convenient for travel than single-piece bows. An archer who hunts as well as target shoots can use the same handle riser with two sets of limbs, rather than use two separate bows, for these pursuits. Also, as a beginner with a take-down bow progresses, he only needs to buy new limbs, instead of a whole new bow, to improve his gear. If you decide to buy a take-down bow, make sure the limbs fit snugly and do not move at the points where they attach to the handle riser.

Whatever bow you choose, the two most important factors in selecting it are its draw weight and its length.

Draw Weight

Bow draw weight is the amount of force needed to pull the bowstring back the length of an arrow. That force is measured in pounds. For easy comparison since arrows come in many lengths, draw weight is always measured with the bowstring drawn back a standard distance of 28 inches. The number of pounds it takes to pull the bowstring back that far is the bow's draw weight. A bow marked 33# @ 28" has a draw weight of 33 pounds. A bow's draw weight will be marked on its handle or lower limb.

Another kind of draw weight is called the actual draw weight. This is the amount of force you exert on the bowstring when you are shooting. Actual draw weight will vary from the draw weight marked on the bow, depending on the length of your draw. Length of draw is determined by holding the bow with an extended arm and drawing the bowstring back until the index finger is under the center of the chin.

Bows are marked at 28 inches. If your draw length is 28 inches, your actual draw weight is the same as the draw weight marked on the bow. If your draw length is less than 28 inches, your actual draw weight is less than the weight marked.

To determine the actual draw weight of your bow, add 2 pounds for every inch over 28 inches you pull back your bowstring, or subtract 2 pounds for every inch under. For example: You have a bow marked 33# @ 28″ (33 pounds at 28 inches), and your draw length is 26 inches. The actual draw weight is 29 pounds, $33 - (2 \text{ inches} \times 2 \text{ pounds})$.

If your father shoots the same bow with a draw length of 29 inches, his actual draw weight is $33 + (1 \text{ inch} \times 2 \text{ pounds})$, or 35 pounds.

A good draw weight to start with is about 25 pounds. This weight will allow you to learn and practice the skills of archery. Archery is not a test of strength but of skill. If your bow is too heavy, you will have a

Parts of the Bow

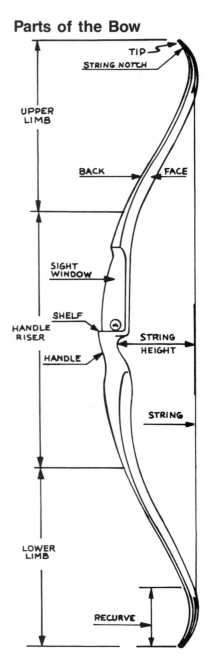

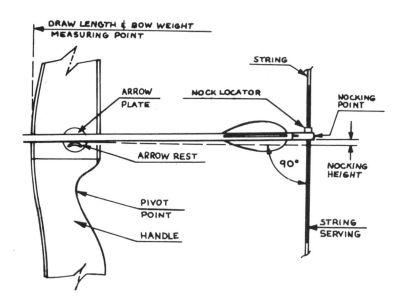

DRAW LENGTH & BOW WEIGHT
MEASURING POINT

STRING

ARROW
PLATE

NOCK LOCATOR

NOCKING
POINT

NOCKING
HEIGHT

ARROW REST

90°

PIVOT
POINT

HANDLE

STRING
SERVING

Proper placement of the arrow on the bow

hard time learning to shoot accurately. You should be able to pull and hold your bow at full draw 10 times for 5 to 10 seconds a time without shaking or getting tired. After you learn the fundamentals of good shooting and you have strengthened your shooting muscles with practice, you may choose to go to a heavier bow.

Bow Length

Bow length is measured by following the contour of the face of the bow from limb tip to limb tip. The bow length is marked on the bow just below the draw weight. An example of a bow lenth is "A.M.O. 64." (A.M.O. stands for the Archery Manufacturers Organization, which sets the standards for bow and string length.)

The length of the bow you choose should depend primarily on the type of shooting you will do. Generally, target bows are longer than those designed for hunting. Typically, target bows are 60 to 70 inches long; hunting bows are 54 to 64 inches long. A rule of thumb is: the longer the bow, the smoother and more accurate the shot; the shorter the bow, the more arrow speed and ease of handling when hunting. A good bow length to start with is about 64 inches.

Care of Your Bow

A bow deserves good care. Always unstring your bow when you are not using it. This will increase its life and prevent it from taking on a permanent bend. Store the unstrung bow in a cool, dry place, hanging it vertically or horizontally on pegs. An occasional coat of furniture wax will protect the finish.

A bow is a delicate instrument. Never use it as a walking stick or allow it to strike objects that will nick or scar it. Scratches can turn into splinters and eventually result in a broken bow. When it might be exposed to rain or possible injury, place the bow in a bow case, a long, narrow sack made of soft material.

Try to avoid drawing your bow farther than your normal draw length. Your bow will develop a set to your draw length, and overdrawing can affect your accuracy.

Always use a bow stringer when stringing your bow. Improper stringing or using step-through or push-pull methods to string can cause permanent damage to your bow. With proper care, your bow will give you many years of pleasure.

The Bowstring and Its Care

The National Archery Association advises beginners to use bowstrings made of Dacron with a serving (a wrapping of thread that protects the bowstring at the point where the arrow is set) made of multifilament nylon thread. Get an expert to help you select a bowstring that is the right length and has the right number of strands for your bow.

You can determine your bowstring's nocking point, the spot where you fit the notched end of the arrow, with a ruler or bow square. (A bow square is a T-shaped device used to measure nocking height and string height.) Lay the shaft of your arrow on the arrow rest and find the point on the string that would place your arrow perpendicular (at a 90-degree angle) to the string. Now measure one-eighth inch up from that spot to find your correct nocking point. This spot should be marked with serving thread, crimp-on nock locator, or something else so that you can find the exact location easily every time.

Keep your bowstring well waxed with either a commercial bowstring wax or one you make yourself using one part resin to three parts beeswax.

Inspect the string carefully before and after each day's shooting. If any of the main strings are broken, discard the whole string. Check the serving and repair or replace it if it is loose or worn. The serving protects the delicate fibers from coming into direct contact with the end of the arrow (arrow nock) and assures longer life of the string. Store the bowstring with your bow.

Selecting Your Arrows

Arrows are generally made from wood, fiberglass, or aluminum, and are fletched (feathered) with either turkey feathers or plastic vanes. (Vanes can refer to a set of feathers, but is more often used to describe fletching made of plastic.) The National Archery Association notes that, generally, feathers are good for indoor archery and beginners, while vanes are good outside because humidity and rain does not affect them.

Wooden arrows are the least expensive, but do not last as long as fiberglass or aluminum. Fiberglass arrows are durable, but wooden and aluminum arrows are lighter and fly faster. Aluminum arrows are a little more expensive, but, with care, they will last a long time.

Today, most archers start with a good wooden arrow. The best wooden arrows are made from Port Orford cedar, a dense, strong, straight-grained wood.

As archers progress in skill, most switch to aluminum. Aluminum arrows are straight, lightweight, and strong. Although they bend, they can often be straightened. Aluminum arrows can be matched perfectly to any bow, and they provide a degree of accuracy superior to wooden or fiberglass arrows.

Types of Arrows

The three types of arrows are target, field, and hunting. Each is designed for a specific use. Target arrows are straight and lightweight and are designed to be used on a target archery range. They have lighter points and smaller feathers than either field or

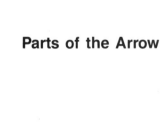

Parts of the Arrow

TYPES OF ARROWS

Target arrows are designed for use with straw targets. They are light, have pointed heads, and are fletched with small feathers.

Field arrows are heavier and have longer feathers than target arrows. Points are shaped for easy removal from various objects.

Hunting arrows are heavier than standard target arrows. They have large feathers and sharply pointed heads with two or more blades.

The rubber-tipped arrow shown may be used for practice or for small game. It should be used as carefully as a hunting arrow.

TYPES OF HEADS

Arrow points or heads are designed for field or target archery or for hunting. Different hunting heads are made for various purposes.

TARGET HEAD   FIELD HEAD   BROADHEAD
(HUNTING HEAD)

hunting arrows. Field arrows are for field archery and hunting small game. They have a distinctive "shouldered" point, and their fletching is usually a little longer than that of target arrows. Hunting arrows are similar to field arrows, but their fletching is a little longer, and they have a three- or four-bladed "broadhead."

Matching Arrows to Your Bow

When you buy your arrows, it is important that you match them to your bow. Matched arrows will fly truer and be more accurate than those that are not. To match arrows to your bow, you must know the draw weight of your bow and the draw length of your arrow. Together, they will determine the spine of the arrow you need. Spine is how stiff an arrow shaft is relative to its thickness, weight, and length.

The draw weight of your bow is marked on its handle. The draw length of your arrow can be measured several ways. The best way to determine correct arrow length is to draw a special measuring arrow that has been marked every inch, like a ruler. When you are at full draw, your correct arrow length is read from the marked arrow where it crosses the back of your bow.

BACK OF BOW

FACE OF BOW

SELECT ARROW LENGTH THAT IS 1" BEYOND THE BACK OF THE BOW

1"

MEASURING ARROW MARKED IN INCHES

Another way to approximate proper arrow length is to stand with both arms extended in front of you, with your finger tips touching. The distance from your finger tips to the base of your neck will give you a close approximation of your correct arrow length.

Try to test a variety of arrows before you buy your own. When you order arrows, be sure to include your bow draw weight, arrow length, and the type of arrow you need: target, field, or hunting. Also include the fletching you want and the type of point you need. With this information, you will be able to get a perfect match for your bow.

Be sure that arrows are long enough for your bow.

15

Remove arrows by bracing the target with one hand and twisting the arrow with the other hand.

Care of Arrows

Arrows must be well cared for. Not only can improper care affect accuracy, but it can also cause injury.

Look for evidence of damage before, during, and after shooting. Start with the nock (the notched end) and work your way to the point. If the nock is cracked or broken, replace it. If your feathers or vanes are coming off, glue them back in place. If your feathers are crushed, they can usually be brought back to shape by holding them over steam from boiling water. The heat and moisture will smooth out the feathers and make the barbs stand erect.

If you are using wooden or fiberglass arrows, check for cracks or splinters. If your arrow is cracked, break it in half and throw it away. If shot, it could explode and cause serious injury. Rough spots in an arrow's finish should be sanded lightly and polished.

Check for loose or dull points. Loose points should be reglued to the shaft. (See chapter titled "Making and Repairing Arrows.") Hone dulled points with a fine file, then clean them with steel wool.

Store your arrows where they will not get wet or be subject to temperature change. Many archers have special cases for storing their arrows. Others keep them in quivers hanging on a wall. Never put anything on top of your arrows; this could damage the fletching and bend the shafts.

Arm Guard

The arm guard protects the arm during shooting by providing a smooth surface for the bowstring to strike. Without an arm guard, your shirt sleeve or skin of your lower arm will often "grab" the bowstring, causing you to shoot low. The arm guard is usually made of tough cordovan leather that is reinforced by a steel band. Adjustable elastic straps hold it snugly over the inside forearm. The hunting arm guard is usually wider and longer than those used on field and target ranges, and has three or four straps instead of two.

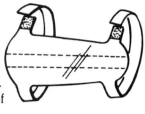

The arm guard is the easiest accessory to select. Almost any commercial brand is suitable. Though absolutely essential, probably no part of the beginner's equipent is so often overlooked.

Arm Guard

Shooting Glove and Tab

Protect your shooting fingers with a shooting glove or tab. Without a glove or tab, your release of the arrow—which is the most crucial motion in shooting—may be faulty. Moreover, even the lightest bow will soon make untrained fingers sensitive, eventually causing blisters. Every student archer should have finger protection no matter how tough he thinks his fingers are. The most experienced and proficient archers always shoot with a glove or tab.

Shooting Glove

This type of finger protection has three finger tips connected to a wrist strap. The glove should fit snugly, but not tightly, over the three shooting fingers. Carefully select a glove that fits well and is comfortable.

Tab

The simplest and most inexpensive finger protection is the tab. Though available in a variety of forms, the tab generally is a loose flap of leather that lies over the fingers that draw the bowstring. As a beginner, you may find the tab awkward, but with a little practice, you can become proficient in using one. Most top target archers use a tab because it provides greater control and a smoother release.

Finger tab

Slings

A number of different styles of slings can be bought or made out of either cord or leather. The two major types are the finger sling and the wrist sling. The finger sling attaches around the thumb and the index finger of the bow hand. Wrist slings are made in two ways: either mounted on the bow and lain across the wrist or looped around the wrist with an end going

Finger sling

around the bow and hooked onto the loop on the inside of the wrist. Try the different styles to see which one works best for you and needs no adjustment after each shot.

Mechanical Release

Mechanical release aids that replace the fingers in holding and releasing the bowstring have increased in use since 1970. The three major types are rope, solid (one-piece), and moving sections.

Since the finger release is an important part of championship form, mechanical releases are not allowed in amateur competition. This ban is in effect at all tournaments sanctioned by the Federation Internationale de Tir a L'Arc (FITA), known in this country as the International Archery Federation, including the Olympics, world championships, and U.S. national championships.

At National Field Archery Association tournaments, release aid shooters are placed in a separate division. Some professional associations also recognize release aids. Exercise exceptional care when using mechanical releases.

Note: The Boy Scouts of America does not recommend the use of mechanical release aids without the strict supervision of a qualified merit badge counselor.

Quivers

Quivers are for carrying or holding reserve arrows. They come in many sizes and shapes, each designed to meet the specific needs or preferences of the archer.

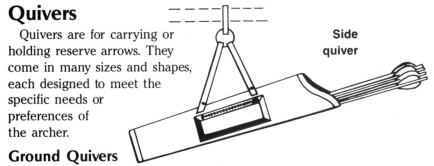

Side quiver

Ground Quivers

These stick in the ground and may include a rack to hold your bow as well as a container for keeping your arrows upright.

Belt Quivers

These attach to your belt and allow you to reach arrows more easily than you can using a ground quiver. Styles include vertical, diagonal, hip, pocket, and holster.

Clothing shield

Back Quivers

These are slung over either shoulder. One drawback to them is that you have to reach high to withdraw an arrow, a problem if you are trying to sneak up on game or are target-shooting in a forested area.

Bow Quivers

These attach to the bow and are convenient for hunters, who have to worry only about carrying one piece of equipment through the brush. Some field archers use bow quivers, but tournament archers usually find them too clumsy to use.

A clothing shield protects clothing from being grabbed by the bowstring after release.

Making the Bowstring

In primitive times, bowstrings were made from raw animal and vegetable fibers. Later, linen came into use because it was strong and did not stretch as much as those fibers, two primary requirements for bowstring material. In recent years, science has developed excellent synthetic fibers, including Dacron, which most beginning archers use for their bowstrings.

Though there are many ways to make a bowstring, the method described here is most commonly used and one of the simplest for a Scout. Work carefully and you will be finished in about an hour. With practice, you can make a bowstring in less than a half-hour.

The Archery Manufacturers Organization (AMO) has standards for bow and string length. The length of all AMO bows is designed to give the proper string height when the bow is braced with a standard $1/16$-inch diameter steel cable.

This cable is exactly 3 inches less than the marked length of the bow. Therefore, a cable for a 66-inch bow is 63 inches.

To make your bowstring, first take a piece of board about 6 feet long and drive a headless nail into one end of it. If you have a spare bowstring, put one end of the string over the nail. Then stretch the string the length of the board and drive a nail into the other end. When the other end of the string is put over the second nail, it should be taut.

If you do not have a spare string to make this measurement, use the AMO standard and place two nails so that they will be 3 inches closer together than the distance between the string grooves (the ends of the bow where the bowstring is fitted) of the unstrung bow.

Now you should have the correct measurement for the string.

An adjustable string jig using two metal posts enables a person to make strings of varying lengths. You can make a very good bowstring using either an adjustable jig or a board with one nail on each end.

Attach your Dacron thread to one of the nails and wind it around the other nail until you have the number of strands the thread package recommends. Or wind until you have 10 strands for a 25-pound bow or 12 strands for a 35-pound bow. Tie the two ends of the thread together and cut off the loose ends.

Next, shift the string on both nails until the knot you have just made is about 1½ inches from one nail. Use the knot as a guide mark; mark the string directly opposite it.

Also make two marks at the other end of the string. These should also be about 1½ inches from their nail. These two sections will form the loops.

Now give the whole string a good coating of wax. Commercial bowstring waxes are easiest to use, but you can make your own with one part resin and three parts beeswax. The wax prevents friction and makes the string last longer.

Next, slip the knot and marks on the string toward the middle of the board until the two sets of marks are opposite each other. You must now separate the two sets of strings. A jig has a specially grooved device to hold them apart, but a small block of wood will do as well.

You are now ready to serve the loops. "Serving" is wrapping thread around the bowstring to protect it from wear. Begin serving your string from the knot toward the mark, which should be at least 3 inches from the knot.

Figure 1 shows how to begin your serving. Lay 3 inches of thread along the string, with the end toward the mark where you will finish, and make your first wrap around the string and over the thread.

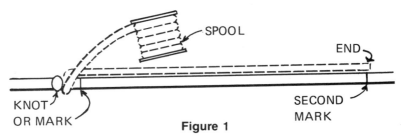

Figure 1

Carefully continue wrapping the serving for about 1 inch, as in figure 2. Then take the other end of the string and pull tightly while holding the wraps with your other hand to ensure a good beginning lock. If you do not hold the wraps securely, they will slip down the string. If they do, you should be able to slip them back to the mark.

Now cut the end of the thread to about one-half inch.

If you have a special "server" (a device for holding the thread), you can now turn the spool tightly, set the slot on the string, and serve down the

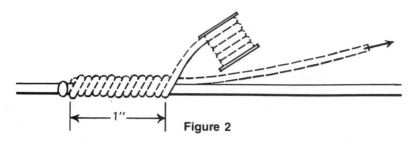

Figure 2

string. A server is easy and quick, but serving can be done just as well by hand by simply laying the serving as you did first.

Serve down the string until you are 1 inch from the finish mark. Now cut off a piece of scrap bowstring thread (Dacron) about 8 inches long. Put some wax on it and lay it on the string as in figure 3 so that the loop is one-half inch past the finish mark.

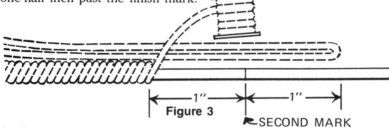

Figure 3

SECOND MARK

Always remember that this loop must be pulled back under the wrapped serving. If you are using a server, be sure to loosen its tension. If not, lay the serving on loosely by hand.

Continue serving over the string and the looped thread until you are four wraps past the finish mark. Pull extra serving off the spool, hold the end of the serving to keep it from unwrapping, and cut off a 4-inch end from the spool. Put about 1½ inches of this end through the thread loop as in figure 4. Take hold of both ends of the thread with one hand. Hold

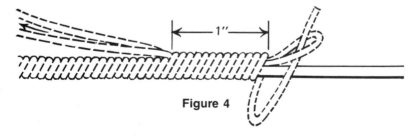

Figure 4

the end wrappings of serving with the other hand and pull the loop with the end of your serving back through the wrapped serving.

To tighten and lock the serving, turn it between your thumb and first finger in the direction it was wrapped, and from the inside to the end, as in figure 5. Any slack will be forced to the outside and can then be tightened by pulling the loose end of the serving. Repeat this procedure until all slack is gone and the serving is tightly locked. Carefully cut the end of the serving loose to the wrapped serving. Your first serving is now complete.

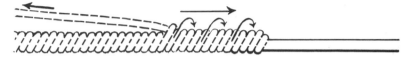

Figure 5

Do the other servings almost the same way. Note that, as in figure 1, when you started next to the knot, you started *inside* it, but when you start with a mark, start *outside* it in order to cover it.

After winding the Dacron thread around the jig, shift the string around the pegs and begin serving the loop (as shown above).

You can use a large steel canvas-repair needle in place of the looped thread (figures 3 and 4). Be sure you put the eye of the needle by the finish mark in place of the loop.

The two marks of the other loop should appear directly across from the serving you just finished. The 3-inch distance between these two marks should be served equal to the one you just completed. Both loop ends will then be done.

Now, shift the string around until the served sections are around the nails. Each end should have the same amount of serving on either side of the nail. The loops are now ready to be closed.

Close the loops by serving the string together for 5 inches down the string. Do this at both ends of the string. Your bowstring is now complete.

With the string on your bow, mark it at a point 2 inches above the arrow rest and 5 inches below it. Serve the area between these marks with the string on the bow. Or you can remove the string and serve it on a string-making board.

This center serving will prevent wear from the arrow nock and your finger gear. Once you have finished this serving, thoroughly wax the whole string.

For future reference, the servings you made were: two loop protections of 3 inches each, two loop closings of 5 inches each, and 7 inches in the center.

Making and Repairing Arrows

Making an arrow requires four steps: putting on the point, the nock, the crest, and fletching.

Point

Putting on a point is the easiest part of making or repairing an arrow. There are three types of point sockets, two for wooden arrows and one for fiberglass or aluminum tubing.

The backs of the points for wooden arrows are hollow and have either parallel or 5-degree-taper walls. The backs of points for tubing shafts are made to insert inside the tubing.

To put the proper-size point on an arrow shaft, you must know the diameter of the shaft.

Cement used on points must be waterproof and strong because the point of an arrow takes most of the force when it hits. Two-part epoxy and heat-weld cements are among the best.

To put a point on a wooden arrow, hold the point with pliers, heat the point over a flame (a candle works well), then melt the glue and allow it to drip into the point. Push the point onto the shaft with the pliers, making sure it is in line with the shaft. Wipe off any excess glue that oozes out from the point and allow the glue to harden and set for a least 12 hours before using the arrow.

To put a point on an aluminum or fiberglass arrow, melt the glue and place some on the point's sleeve (the part that fits into the arrow shaft). Insert the point into the shaft and then push the point hard against a firm surface. Wipe off any excess glue that oozes out and allow it to harden and set for several hours.

To remove a loose or damaged point, rotate the arrow over a flame—heat the point on a wooden arrow and heat the shaft just behind the point on an aluminum or fiberglass arrow, making sure not to put any part of the arrow in the flame. Remove the point with pliers.

Nock

Putting the nock on a bare shaft is also easy. All nocks have an 11-degree inside taper. Tubing shafts have a special insert with the proper taper to receive the nock.

In replacing a broken nock, you must position the new nock so that its string slot is perpendicular to the cock or guide feather.

Cement used on nocks must be waterproof. It can be the quick-drying type.

Crest

The crest is your identifying marks on your arrows. A crest should be close enough to the fletching so that it does not get buried in the target, but it should be at least 5 centimeters (2 inches) from the end of the fletching.

Design and color your crest as you wish. If you buy ready-made arrows, you may want to add a color or design that identifies them as yours.

Fletching

The term *fletch* comes from the French word *fleche,* which means arrow. Fletching an arrow means applying feathers to the shaft. Proper fletching is critical for an arrow to fly true and be accurate.

Arrows can be fletched with either turkey feathers or plastic vanes. Turkey feathers can be purchased dyed and cut to size. In the past, turkey feathers were purchased whole and had to be cut or burned to the proper shape.

TARGET ARROW

Shape of feathers may vary depending on type of arrow. Target and field arrow fletching are illustrated here.

FIELD ARROW

It is important that you use only right-wing or left-wing feathers on a single arrow. If you mix the feathers, the arrow will not fly true.

Many archers prefer to use plastic vanes instead of feathers. Vanes are more precise than feathers and last much longer. In addition, vanes are not affected by moisture or weather changes. Plastic vanes are used by both target and field archers and are available in flexible and rigid materials.

The size and shape of your fletching will depend on the type of shooting you will do. In general, hunting and field arrows have longer fletching than target arrows do. Longer fletching helps stabilize the greater head weight of the shaft, which is due to the heavier points used in field archery and bow hunting. Target arrows normally have fletching from 2 to 3 inches long. Field and hunting arrows are fletched with feathers or vanes up to 5 inches long.

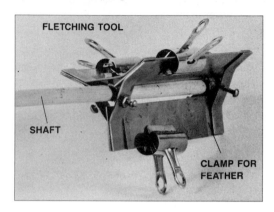

FLETCHING TOOL

SHAFT

CLAMP FOR FEATHER

In most cases, experienced archers experiment with many sizes before settling on one with which they feel most comfortable.

Whether you use feathers or plastic vanes, the process of fletching an arrow is the same. The materials you will need are arrow shafts, nocks, feathers or vanes, a fletching jig, glue, and some rubbing alcohol.

First, clean the end of the shaft with some rubbing alcohol and a clean rag. It is important you keep the area you are working on free of dirt and of oils from your hands. The glue sticks better to a clean surface.

After cleaning the shaft end, install a nock. Use only one drop of glue to hold the nock in place and be sure it goes on straight. More glue will cause the nock to get soft and warp out of alignment.

Next, place your arrow shaft in the fletching jig. Some fletching jigs allow you to attach all three sets of feathers at the same time, and some, only one at a time. Locate the clamp on a three-feather jig that will hold the cock feather or guide feather, or set your one-feather jig to the correct position. The cock feather is set perpendicular (at a 90-degree angle) to the slot in the nock and is often a different color from the other two feathers or vanes.

Place a feather or vane in the jig clamp. If you are using plastic vanes, wipe the base of the vane with some rubbing alcohol to remove any oils from the plastic. Apply a thin bead of glue to the entire base of the vane and wipe off any excess. Be careful not to get glue on the sides of the fletching or the clamp.

Now slide the clamp into position in the jig until the base of the feather rests snugly against the shaft. Do not move the feather or clamp again until the glue is dry. Drying usually takes about 20 minutes.

Repeat this procedure until all feathers are in place. When they are, remove the arrow from the jig, then place a small drop of glue on each end of the fletchings and set the arrow aside to dry one more time. These last drops of glue make your fletching job last much longer by keeping the ends of your fletching from coming loose.

The procedure for repairing an arrow is the same as for fletching a new one. The trick is to be sure the arrow is properly positioned in the jig to accept the correct feather.

In the past, fletching with feathers was much more difficult. The archer had to split, cut, and trim all his own feathers. Wire burners to shape feathers made the job easier, but it was still a lot of work.

Today, feathers are precut and come in many different colors. But it is still possible to special order uncut, natural turkey feathers. If you enjoyed fletching your arrows, you might try natural feathers next time for a little extra challenge.

Shooting Techniques

Shooting a bow involves nine basic steps: stance, nock, extend, draw, anchor, tighten and hold, aim, release, follow-through.

The techniques described here are for right-handed archers. Left-handed archers should reverse body positions.

Before you begin shooting, check your bow from time to time by sighting down the limbs. The string should go straight down the middle of both limbs.

If your bow has a twisted limb, let an experienced adult archer fix it.

When you string your bow, also check the string height (fistmele). The string height is the distance between the handle and the string when the bow is strung.

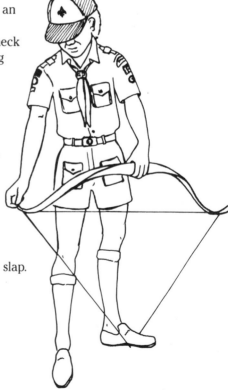

The correct string height is set by the manufacturer. On most modern bows it is from 7 to 9 inches (17.7 to 22.8 centimeters). If your bowstring is too short, there will be too much string height and your bow limbs will be under too much strain. If the bowstring is too long, there will be too little string height, and it may give you a lot of arm and wrist slap.

Use a stringer to string your bow each time. The illustration shows the proper way to string straight and recurved bows. Improper stringing can damage or twist a bow's limbs.

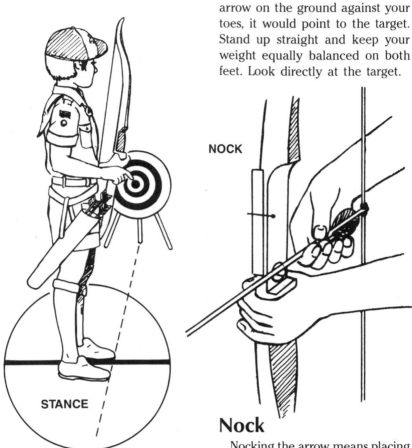

arrow on the ground against your toes, it would point to the target. Stand up straight and keep your weight equally balanced on both feet. Look directly at the target.

NOCK

Stance

Your stance is the position you assume when you shoot. Your body should be parallel to the flight of the arrow, with your left side toward the target. Stand comfortably, keeping your feet about shoulders' width apart. Touch your toes to an imaginary line leading to the center of the target. If you were to lay an

Nock

Nocking the arrow means placing the arrow on the string and the bow. With your right hand, lay the shaft of the arrow on the arrow rest and nock the arrow (fit the notched end on the string) just below the string's nocking point. Be sure the cock (odd-colored) feather is facing away from the bow.

Keep your shoulders level. Lightly grip the bow with its weight against the base of your thumb.

Center the bow's pressure in the "Y" formed by your thumb and index finger. Avoid a tight "death grip" on the bow handle because a tight grip chokes the natural action of the bow.

EXTEND

Extend

Seat your left hand (if you are right-handed) comfortably in the handle of the bow. Raise your left arm and the bow until the bow is pointed directly at the target. At the same time, rotate your left elbow downward so that it will not be in the way of the string when you release.

Draw

With your right hand, reach out and place three fingers on the bowstring, index finger above the arrow and middle two fingers below it. The string should rest in the first joint of all three fingers. Your right hand is now forming a "hook" on the bowstring, and your left hand lightly holds the handle.

Keeping your left arm fully extended and your left shoulder down, begin to draw the bowstring with your right hand. Your right hand and elbow should stay at shoulder level. Your right forearm becomes a straightline extension of the arrow. Use your strong back muscles to draw the bow, concentrating on smoothly and steadily moving your elbow straight back. Be sure to draw your bow the same length each time.

(Example shown on following page.)

DRAW

Anchor

The anchor point is where the archer's hand and bowstring touches the face at full draw. It is extremely important that you use the same anchor point for every shot. The anchor point serves the same function as the rear sight on a rifle. A sloppy anchor is the same as a loose sight.

The two basic anchors are the "under-the-chin" anchor most target archers use and the "side-of-the-face" anchor most bow hunters use. Beginners are advised to start with the "under-the-chin" anchor because it calls for consistency and can be easily checked. Also, it allows for easier string alignment and more accurate shooting.

ANCHOR

As you reach full draw, your head will rest on top of your hand. Your index finger will contact your jaw bone, forming a solid contact point. The bowstring will touch the tip of your nose and the center of your chin. These three contact points make this anchor solid and reliable.

Tighten and Hold

Once you have established your anchor, tighten your back and hold the bow steady. Maintain this tension. You need it to keep the proper anchor and a consistent draw length.

Aim

Two basic methods are used for aiming a bow: bow sight and point of aim. Bow sight is more accurate and easier to learn.

Whatever method of aiming you use, be sure to hold until you are sure of a good shot. Snap shooting, releasing too quickly, does not allow you to aim properly and can lead to problems later. Take your time, aim well, and then shoot.

Bow Sight

To shoot effectively with a bow sight, you must learn to come to full draw and hold the sight pin dead center on the target. Make sure your anchor is solid. Once at full draw, look past the string and you will see the sight pin and the target. One or the other will be out of focus. It does not matter which one is in focus; concentrate on the one you feel most comfortable with.

Bow sights of all kinds are available. Some are simple pins used for hunting, while others are complex and used for advanced target competition.

All sights work the same way. The only difference in them is that some are more easily adjustable for different distances.

To start, try a simple pin or target-type sight. You can make your own. Place a strip of foam tape on the back of your bow. Then put a straight pin in the tape in such a way that it is visible on the arrow side of the bow. Or tape a larger eraser with a straight point protruding from it to the sight window.

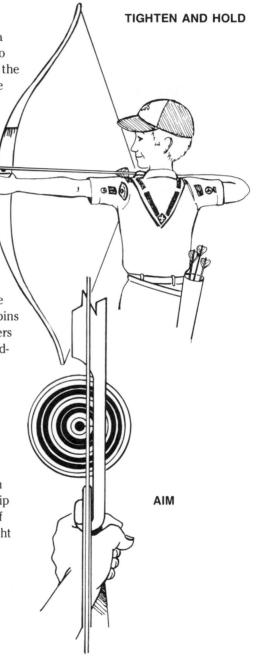

AIM

34

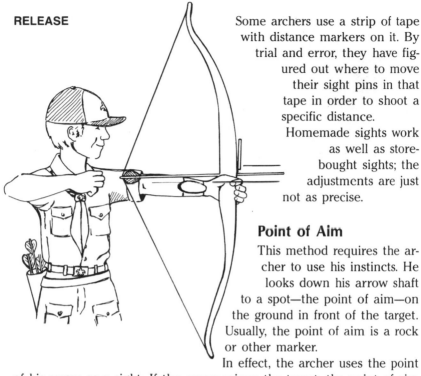

RELEASE

Some archers use a strip of tape with distance markers on it. By trial and error, they have figured out where to move their sight pins in that tape in order to shoot a specific distance.

Homemade sights work as well as store-bought sights; the adjustments are just not as precise.

Point of Aim

This method requires the archer to use his instincts. He looks down his arrow shaft to a spot—the point of aim—on the ground in front of the target. Usually, the point of aim is a rock or other marker.

In effect, the archer uses the point of his arrow as a sight. If the arrow misses the target, the point of aim marker is moved, either up or back, until the arrow strikes the target center.

Release

Releasing is simply a matter of relaxing the fingers that hold the string while you maintain the tension in your back. When your draw fingers relax, the string will escape, and the arrow will be on its way. Before you release, run a quick mental check of all the other steps. If everything is right, release, and you will see your arrow strike the bull's-eye.

Follow-through

As you release, maintain your good shooting form and keep your eyes on the target. Try to move as little as possible. Some people count to three before they relax. Movement during follow-through can cause an otherwise good shot to miss the mark. In a good follow-through, your right hand

FOLLOW-THROUGH

will be at the back of your neck, and your bow arm will still be lined up perfectly with the target.

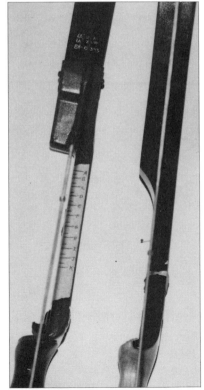

Types of sights

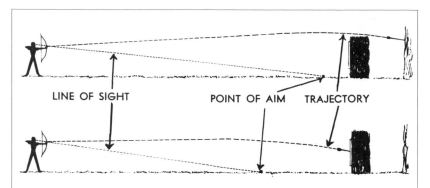

LINE OF SIGHT   POINT OF AIM   TRAJECTORY

At full draw, the archer looks over the tip of the arrow at a marker between him and the target. In the top illustration, the point of aim is too far from the archer; the arrow misses the target completely. By moving the marker and changing the point of aim, the archer can achieve an accurate trajectory.

Rounds

An archery tournament is made up of one or more rounds. Each round consists of a series of arrows shot at specified distances and target faces. Tournaments can last from a few hours to several days.

Competitive archery is broken into two styles, target and field. Target archery is shot with a recurve bow on a large, open field, with multi-colored target faces. This is the type of archery shot in the Olympics and world championships. Field archery is shot on a roving course. Archers use compound bows and shoot at different angles and distances. Field archery is said to be an approximation of bow hunting.

Tournament rules are made by these four organizations:

- National Field Archery Association (NFAA), which since 1946 has developed American field archery rounds for amateur and professional competition. The NFAA is a member of the International Field Archery Association and is headquartered at R.D. 2 Box 514, Redlands, CA 92373.
- National Archery Association (NAA), which since 1879 has set up American amateur target archery rounds and since 1960 has approved international amateur target and field rounds for Americans in Olympic and FITA competition. A member of the International Archery Federation and the U.S. Olympic Committee, the NAA is headquartered at 1750 East Boulder Street, Colorado Springs, CO 80909.
- International Archery Federation (FITA), which since 1931 has set up international amateur rounds and since 1970 has coordinated archery in the Olympics. Its Executive Bureau is located at Via G. B. Piranesi 44/b, I—20137, Milan, Italy.
- Professional Archers Association (PAA), which since 1961 has set up American professional rounds for cash prizes. It is headquartered at P.O. Box 24407, Mayfield Heights, OH 44124. PAA rounds are not covered in this pamphlet.

Field Archery and Target Archery

Field archery is set up on a course or roving range. Different target faces and shooting distances are used for 14 targets. Stakes are driven into the ground to mark the exact shooting spot for each target, and the archer stands behind the stakes.

The field, hunter's, animal, Scout field, and Flint rounds are all field rounds. In NFAA competition, Junior Division archers are grouped by age and type of shooting: Cubs (less than 12 years old), Youth (12–15), and Young Adult (16–17). Adults (18 and over) are grouped by type of shooting.

Flights are set up within each division based on each archer's handicap, just as handicaps are given in golf and bowling.

In target archery, the archers are grouped by age: Cadet (less than 12 years old), Junior (12–14), Intermediate (15–17), and Adult (18 and over). Adults are also classified by their scores as Class C, B, A, or AA.

The outdoor target course is set up in an open field, using 122-centimeter (48-inch) target faces. In most cases, the target is set and the firing line is moved for different distances. The longest distances are shot first.

For indoor target archery rounds, 60- or 40-centimeter targets are used.

The 900, Junior 900, Easton, Junior Easton, and FITA Indoor rounds I and II are standard target rounds.

The NAA Junior Olympic Archery Development rounds are special target rounds used by JOAD clubs.

Target archers straddle the firing line, with one foot over and one foot behind the line.

Field Round (NFAA and FITA International)

The field round, originally developed to give archers a way to practice bow hunting, has become as much a game as it is hunting practice.

The course is set up in the woods, using 14 targets that vary in size from 6 to 24 inches.

Four arrows are shot at each target. For 11 of the targets, the four arrows are shot from the same distance, but position varies from a different distance. Distances and target sizes are listed below.

Distances are marked by white stakes. They do not follow in any special order and may be arranged as best suits the terrain.

On the FITA target, the bull's-eye is one-half the diameter of the total scoring area. In the center is a black dot called an "aiming spot." The targets are black and white. The white bull is scored as 5 points and the white outer ring as 3 points.

The NFAA targets are larger than the FITA targets and have five scoring rings. The black center spot is one-fifth of the outer diameter of the target and has an inner circle half the diameter of the spot. This is used in breaking tied scores.

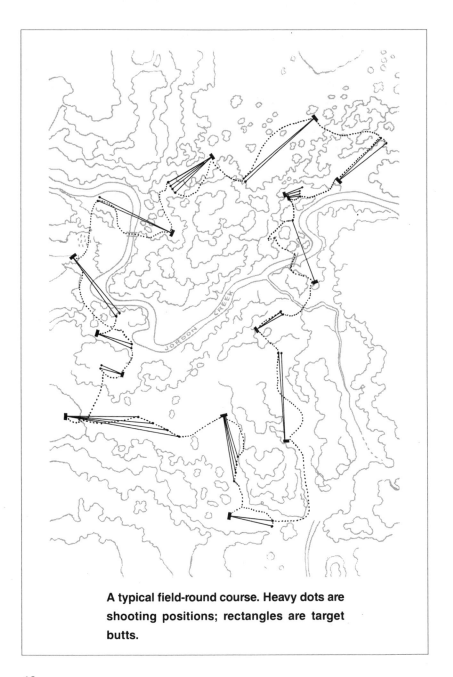

A typical field-round course. Heavy dots are shooting positions; rectangles are target butts.

Standard field round scoring is 5 points for the black bull's-eye, 4 for the outer black area.

NFAA COURSE

DISTANCE		TARGET SIZE	
Meters	Yards	Centimeters	Inches
73-64-55-45.6	80-70-60-50	65	26
59.5	65	65	26
55	60	65	26
50	55	65	26
45.6	50	50	20
41.2-36.6-32-27.4	45-40-35-30	50	20
41.2	45	50	20
36.6	40	50	20
32-32-32-32	35-35-35-35	50	20
27.4	30	35	12
22.9	25	35	12
18.3	20	35	12
13.7	15	35	12
10.7-9-7.5-6	35-30-25-20 feet	20	8

FITA COURSE

DISTANCE	TARGET SIZE
Meters	Centimeters
60-55-50-45	60
60	60
55	60
45	45
45-40-35-30	45
40	45
35	45
35-35-35-35	45
30	30
25	30
20	30
15	30
12-10-8-6	15

Hunter's Round (NFAA and FITA International)

The hunter's round is designed to give the archer practice in concentrating on the target area. Shooting distances are slightly less than in the field

The diagram shows the positions, distances, and target sizes for the official NFAA Boy Scout field round. The course may be set up in camps where there is little space for archery.

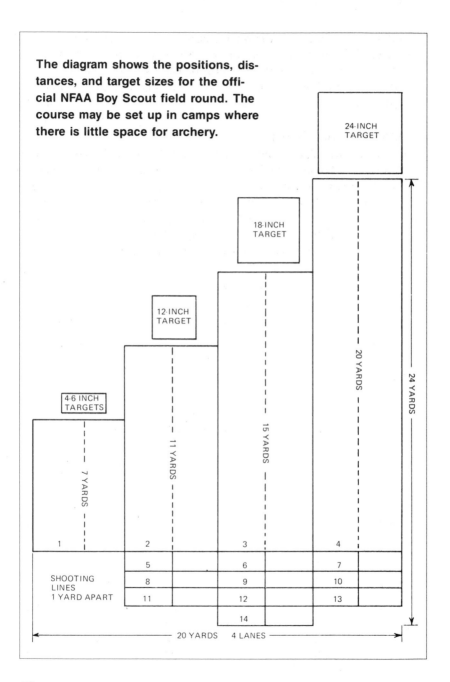

round, but the NFAA uses the same courase, with red stakes and marked distances. FITA uses a separate course with more random, unmarked distances. Archers must change positions for each shot in a hunter's round.

Scoring is 5 for the bull and 3 for the outer ring, the same as in a field round.

Animal Round (NFAA)

The animal round, designed for bow hunting practice, is laid out on the same course as the field and hunter's rounds. However, animal target faces are used instead of the circular black-and-white targets. Targets have two scoring areas, the "vital" kill and the "nonvital." Three arrows may be used for each target. The first arrow to hit scores, and any remaining arrows are not scored. Thus, if the first arrow hits the target, the second and third are not scored. Scoring is shown below. If all three arrows miss—no score.

ANIMAL ROUND

HIT	VITAL AREA	NONVITAL AREA
First arrow	20 points	16 points
Second arrow	14 points	10 points
Third arrow	8 points	4 points

CUB ROUND (NFAA)

DISTANCE		FIELD		HUNTER	
Meters	Yards	Centimeters	Inches	Centimeters	Inches
7.6	20 feet	20	8	20	8
9	10 yards	35	12	35	12
9	10	35	12	35	12
9	10	35	12	35	12
9	10	35	12	35	12
13.7	15	50	20	35	12
16.2	18	50	20	50	20
18.3	20	50	20	50	20
18.3	20	50	20	50	20
18.3	20	50	20	50	20
18.3	20	50	20	50	20
22.9	25	65	26	65	26
27.4	30	65	26	65	26
27.4	30	65	26	65	26

Freeman Round (NFAA)

This round consists of 60 arrows shot as three games at distances of 9, 13.5, and 18 meters (10, 15, and 20 yards). Each game includes four ends of five arrows.

First Game—Three ends at 9 meters (10 yards); one end at 13.5 meters (15 yards).

Second Game—Three ends at 13.5 meters (15 yards); one end at 18 meters (20 yards).

Third Game—Four ends at 18 meters (20 yards).

The target is the standard NFAA indoor target of 40 centimeters with a blue-and-white face and 8-centimeter bull's-eye, scored 5, 4, 3, 2, 1.

Indoor Round (NFAA)

This consists of 60 arrows shot as three games at a distance of 18 meters (20 yards). Each game has four ends of five arrows per end.

The target and scoring are the same as in the NFAA Freeman Round.

Scout Field Round (BSA)

The Scout field round is a scaled-down version of the field round. It requires less space and can be set up in a confined area in camp. It can also be set up as a regular roving field course. Scoring is the same as in standard field archery, and the same target faces are used.

Four arrows are shot at each target.

FLINT ROUND (20-yard) (NFAA)

TARGET	DISTANCE		TARGET SIZE	
	Meters	Feet	Centimeters	Inches
1	15	50	35	12
2	6	20	20	8
3	18.3	60	35	12
4	13.7	45	20	8
5	12	40	35	12
6	9	30	20	8
7	18.3-15-12-9	60-50-40-30	35	12

10-ring target

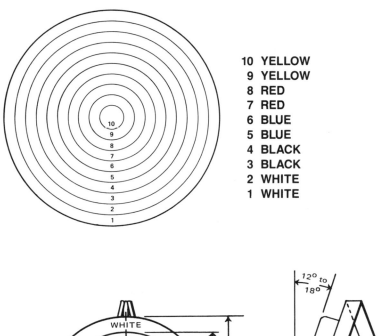

10 **YELLOW**
9 **YELLOW**
8 **RED**
7 **RED**
6 **BLUE**
5 **BLUE**
4 **BLACK**
3 **BLACK**
2 **WHITE**
1 **WHITE**

Layout of an official archery target (portable)

Name	JOHN SCOUT							Name	ANDY STAR							
Address	67 ARROW DRIVE							Address	10 QUIVER ROAD							
BRUNSWICK, MAINE								BRUNSWICK, MAINE								
Date 04-12-77 Round JOAD								Date 4-12-77 Round Jr. 900								
Target 2 Archer 3								Target 8 Archer 2								
CLASSIFICATION - CADET								CLASSIFICATION - JUNIOR								

Left — JOHN SCOUT

						Hits	Score
9	6	4	4			4	23
7	4					2	11
6	5	4	2	1		5	18
6	2	1				3	9
7	6					2	13
25 METERS						16	74
6	6	5	5			4	22
8	5	5	2	2		5	22
9	4	3				3	16
8	5	4	2			4	19
9						1	9
25 METERS						17	88
8	7	7	5	4		5	31
4	3	2				3	9
9	7	6	6	1		5	28
9	9	8	7	2		4	32
5	2	2	2	2		5	13
25 METERS						22	113

HITS SCORE
score SEE ABOVE

Right — ANDY STAR

							Hits	Score
6	5	3	1				4	15
6	4	3	2				4	15
7	5	2	2				4	16
7	5	5	3	3			5	23
8	5	3	2	2			5	20
50 METERS							22	89
8	4	3	3	1			5	19
8	5	5	4	3	1		6	26
9	7	6	2	1			5	25
9	6	5	2				4	22
8	5	5	3	2	1		6	24
40 METERS							26	116
10	9	6	5	3	2		6	35
10	8	5	5	4	2		6	34
9	8	6	4	3			5	30
8	7	5	5	4	4		6	33
8	8	7	7	4	3		6	37
30 METERS							29	169

HITS SCORE
score 77 374

SCOUT FIELD ROUND (BSA)

POSITION	DISTANCE		TARGET SIZE	
	Meters	Yards	Centimeters	Inches
1	6.4	7	15.2	6
2	10	11	30.5	12
3	13.7	15	45.8	18
4	18.3	20	61	24
5	11	12	30.5	12
6	14.6	16	45.8	18
7	19.4	21	61	24
8	11.9	13	30.5	12
9	15.5	17	45.8	18
10	20	22	61	24
11	12.8	14	30.5	12
12	16.5	18	45.8	18
13	21	23	61	24
14	17.4	19	45.8	18

900 Round (NAA)

This is an outdoor target round. The course is set up in an open area. A 122-centimeter (48-inch) five-color target with 10-ring scoring is used.

Scoring, from center out, is 10-9-8-7-6-5-4-3-2-1. The distances and number of arrows are:

30 arrows at 60 meters
30 arrows at 50 meters
30 arrows at 40 meters

They are shot in "ends" of six arrows. This means that the score is checked after each six arrows have been shot.

Junior 900 Round (NAA)

This is similar to the 900 round. The target face and scoring are the same; the distances are shorter. Distances and numbers of arrows are:

30 arrows at 50 meters
30 arrows at 40 meters
30 arrows at 30 meters

Easton Round (NAA)

A 122-centimeter (48-inch) target is used with 10-ring scoring. It is shot in ends of five arrows.
20 arrows at 60 meters
20 arrows at 50 meters
20 arrows at 40 meters

Junior Easton Round (NAA)

A 122-centimeter (48-inch) target is used with 10-ring scoring. It is shot in ends of five arrows.
20 arrows at 50 meters
20 arrows at 40 meters
20 arrows at 30 meters

Indoor FITA Round I (NAA and FITA International)

A five-color target face is used, with 10-ring scoring: 10-9-8-7-6-5-4-3-2-1. The target has a 40-centimeter face. Thirty arrows are shot at 18 meters. It is shot in ends of three arrows.

Indoor FITA Round II (NAA and FITA International)

This is similar to FITA Round I, with 30 arrows shot. However, the distance is 25 meters, and the target has a 60-centimeter face. Shot in ends of three arrows.

Junior Olympic Archery Development (NAA)

The Junior Olympic Archery Development (JOAD) program of the NAA is a system that classifies young archers by their scores. The ratings are Yeoman, Junior Bowman, Bowman, Junior Archer, Archer, Master Archer, Expert Archer, and Olympian.

Outdoor shooting distances are 15, 20, 25, 30, 40, 60, and 70 meters. Outdoor qualifying rounds are shot in ends of six at 122-centimeter (48-inch) targets.

The indoor distance is 18 meters. Qualifying rounds are shot in ends of six at 60-centimeter faces with progressively higher scores required for advancement.

All JOAD qualifying rounds use the five-color target with 10-ring scoring.

International and Olympic Shooting

After you have earned your Archery merit badge, you may wish to try your skills in a tournament. Local clubs put on tournaments for both target and field shooters. You may even set your sights on national, international, or even Olympic competition.

Olympic and world archery titles are governed by the Federation Internationale de Tir a L'Arc (FITA), known in this country as the International Archery Federation. FITA consists of delegates from member nations and makes all decision concerning equipment, rules of conduct, and every other aspect concerning tournament archery.

The recognized championship round for national and international archery tournaments is called the FITA. The FITA is shot in groups of 36 arrows at four distances, marked off in meters. FITA distances are: Gentlemen—90, 70, 50, and 30 meters; Ladies—70, 60, 50, and 30 meters. The longer distances are always shot first.

Shooting may be completed in one or two days. In most international tournaments, including the Olympics, competition consists of two FITA rounds shot over four days. In tournaments where the FITA round is shot along with other rounds, the FITA round is always shot first.

In the FITA, two different-size target faces are used. At the longer two distances, a 122-centimeter face is used. At the shorter two, an 80-centimeter face is used. Both faces have five color zones, gold, red, blue, black, and white. Each zone is divided into two areas by a scoring line, making a total of 10 scoring zones.

These zones are worth from 10 points to 1 point, starting in the center at 10 and working outward to 1. The highest score possible on a single FITA round is 1,440.

To qualify for U.S. Olympic tryouts, men must shoot at last three scores of 1,100 and women at least three scores of 1,050 in sanctioned tournaments. The highest possible score would be 1,440 with 144 arrows.

Archery Terms

ANCHOR POINT. The point on an archer's face which the index finger or drawing hand touches during the act of holding and aiming.

ARCHERY GOLF. Adaption of the use of the bow and arrow to the game of golf.

ARM GUARD. A piece of leather or other material worn on the arm holding the bow to protect the forearm from being slapped by the bowstring after release.

ARROWHEAD. The tip of an arrow, designed to protect the front end of the shaft or to aid in killing.

ARROWPLATE. A piece of material that is glued to the side of the bow at the point where the arrow contacts it. It provides protection for the bow from the friction of the arrow. Some modern bows have adjustable arrowplates to help tune the bow more precisely.

ARROW REST. A small protrusion on the bow at the point where the arrow will rest during the draw.

BACK. The outer side of the bow, farthest away from the string.

BARBS. The two sharp points of an arrowhead that project backward.

BARE BOW. The style of shooting that does not allow for the use of sights, stabilizers, or other shooting aids.

BOW ARM. The arm that holds the bow while shooting.

BOW SIGHT. A sighting device attached to the bow.

BOW SQUARE. A device, usually T-shaped, used to measure string height and nocking height.

BOWYER. One who makes bows.

BRACE. To string a bow.

BROADHEAD. A hunting point with two or more cutting edges.

BUTT. Any material designed to stop arrows. A target face is pinned on the butt.

CAST. The distance a bow can shoot an arrow.

CLOUT. A white object, such as a cloth, that is placed on a stake as a mark for long-distance shooting.

COCK FEATHER. The feather that is at right angles to the bow during the draw; usually the odd-colored feather. Also known as a guide feather.

COMPOSITE BOW. A bow made of more than one substance.

COMPOUND BOW. A bow developed in recent years that uses a system of cams, pulleys, and cables to change the weight build-up as the bowstring is drawn. Peak draw weight occurs during the first few inches of draw, with a reduction of up to 50 percent at full draw. Compound bows must be used in all NFAA and FITA competition.

CREEP. To let the arrow move forward after reaching full draw, but before release. Creep is caused by a loss of back tension.

CREST. The decoration of an arrow, usually consisting of several bands of color. It is used for identification.

CROSSBOW. A bow designed to be shot similarly to a gun, with a groove or barrel that directs the arrow and a trigger that releases the string.

DRAW. The act of pulling back the bowstring.

DRAWING ARM. The arm that draws the bowstring.

DRAW WEIGHT. The amount of pull, measured in pounds, needed to draw an arrow back its full length. For easy comparison of bows, draw weight is always measured with the bowstring drawn back a standard distance of 28 inches. Also known as bow weight.

END. The number of arrows shot before the score is taken. In target archery, the number is usually six, sometimes three. In field archery, it is usually four, sometimes three.

FACE. The scoring surface on a target. It is made of paper, canvas, oil cloth, or other material. Also, the side of the bow nearest the string.

FINGER SLING. A strap attached to the thumb and index finger of the bow hand and used to keep the bow from falling after an arrow's release.

FISTMELE. The traditional term for string height. Fistmele was measured by placing the fist on the bow handle and raising the thumb toward the string. It is not applicable to most modern bows.

FLETCH. To put feathers or plastic vanes on the arrow near its nock.

FLETCHER. One who puts feathers or vanes on an arrow. Also used to designate the jig used in placing feathers on the arrow for cementing.

FLIGHT ARROW. A light arrow used in shooting for distance.

FLIGHT BOW. A bow designed for maximum cast with little consideration for accuracy.

FLU-FLU. An arrow used to shoot aerial disc targets or for hunting birds. It has very large feathers, which slow it rapidly after the first 30 yards and cause it to drop quickly.

FREESTYLE. In target archery, shooting that does not allow the use of release aids or optical sights. In field archery, shooting with any approved shooting aid.

GLOVE. Three leather fingers held on the first three fingers of the release hand with a wrist strap. It protects the archer's fingers.

GUIDE FEATHER. *See* COCK FEATHER

HANDLE. The rigid center portion of the bow that is held during shooting.

HEAD. The point or tip of the arrow.

HIT. To strike the target for a score.

HOLDING. Keeping an arrow at full draw while aiming.

INSTINCTIVE SHOOTING. Shooting without the aid of a sighting device or point-of-aim.

KISSER BUTTON (KISSER). A marker placed on the bowstring so that it touches the archer's lips when he is at full draw. It helps establish a better anchor point.

LAMINATE. To build or cover in thin layers. A laminated bow is a composite bow made of several layers of material glued together.

LET DOWN. To slowly release tension from full draw without losing the arrow.

LIMB. The upper or lower portion of the bow that bend when the bowstring is drawn.

LONGBOW. A straight bow that has only one curve when strung.

NOCK. The notched part of the arrow that is fitted to the bowstring. Also, to secure the arrow on the string before drawing.

NOCKING POINT. The point on the bowstring where the notched end of the arrow, the nock, is fitted. It is often marked by extra serving or nock locators.

NOCK LOCATOR. An attachment to the center serving of a bowstring used to mark the nocking point. It may be a metal crimp-on, a piece of plastic that shrinks to fit, or additional serving.

OVERBOWED. Equipped with too strong a bow.

OVERDRAW. To draw an arrow so far that the point passes the face of the bow.

PERFECT END. In target archery, six arrows shot consecutively into the gold zone.

POINT-BLANK. The distance at which the point-of-aim and the center of the target are the same.

POINT OF AIM. A method of aiming in which the archer sights down his arrow shaft at a marker, usually an object on the ground, to try to hit the target. Also, the object used as the marker.

QUIVER. A container for holding arrows.

RANGE. Distance to be shot; a shooting ground, indoors or out.

RECURVE BOW. A bow that when unstrung bends in the opposite direction from its curve when strung. When strung, its tips tend to curve back in reverse to its body.

RELEASE. To let the bowstring escape from the finger tips, thus sending the arrow on its way.

ROUND. A series of arrows shot at specified target faces at set distances.

ROVING. Shooting at random objects at unknown distances.

SERVING. A wrapping of thread around the bowstring to protect it where the arrow is nocked and where the loops contact the bow's string grooves.

SHAFT. The main body of the arrow.

SHOOTING LINE. A line a specified distance from the target. In field archery, the shooter stands behind it; in target archery, he straddles it.

SIGHT PIN. An indicator an archer puts on his bow and uses as an aid in aiming.

SIGHT WINDOW. The cut-away section of the bow above its handle.

SPINE. The stiffness of an arrow shaft in relation to its thickness weight, and length.

STABILIZER. A weighted rod screwed into the bow to help steady it and minimize undesirable twisting of the bow or bowstring.

STRING FINGERS. The three fingers used to draw the bowstring.

STRING GROOVES. The two ends of the bow where the bowstring is fitted. Also known as string nocks.

STRING HEIGHT. The distance between the bow's handle and bowstring when the bow is strung. It is set by the manufacturer and is usually from 7 to 9 inches.

STRUNG BOW. A bow that is ready for shooting; also called a braced bow.

TAB. A flat piece of leather or plastic worn on the drawing hand to protect the fingers when drawing the string and to ensure a smooth release.

TACKLE. Any or all of an archer's equipment.

TASSEL. A large piece of yarn worn on the archer's belt and used to wipe arrows clean.

TORQUE. An undesirable twisting of the bow or bowstring on release.

TOXOPHILITE. An archer or one who is interested in all aspects of archery, including its history.

TRAJECTORY. The path of the arrow in flight.

VANE. The feathers or plastic substitutes that act as rudders in steering the arrow.

WAND. A slat 2 inches wide and 6 inches long shot at from a distance of 100 yards.

WEIGHT OF BOW. *See* DRAW WEIGHT.

WRIST SLING. A strap attached to the bow and wrist of the archer's bow hand and used to keep the bow from falling after an arrow's release.

Books About Archery

Recommended by the American Library Association's Advisory Committee to Scouting.

Barrett, Jean A. *Archery.* 2d ed. Goodyear, 1973.
Briefly describes equipment, fundamental skills, rating sheets, terminology, and types of competition.

Burke, Edmund H. *Archery Handbook.* Arco, 1954.
Interesting reading on techniques, tricks, the approach to field and target archery and instructions for making a flight bow and crossbow.

Campbell, Donald W. *Archery.* Prentice-Hall, 1971.
A compact volume with good tips on equipment, mechanics, and tournaments, including a chapter on physical conditioning.

Colby, C. B. *First Bow and Arrow.* Coward, 1955.
A beginner's book covering identification of bow and arrow parts, archery accessories, instructions for repair, and the careful use of equipment.

Gillelan, G. Howard. *Archery.* Cornerstone, 1972.
An explanation of accessories the beginner will need and a stress on safety in their use.

Hamilton, T. M. *Native American Bows.* 2d ed. Shumway, 1982.
For the student of history, this explores the aboriginal American bow, dart, and arrow; their effectiveness and construction.

Henderson, Al. *Understanding Winning Archery.* Target Communications Corp., 1983
How to get involved in tournament archery, including what it takes and how to get there.

Hougham, Paul C. *The Encyclopedia of Archery.* Barnes, 1958.
A comprehensive treatment of the history and mechanics of archery including diagrammed explanations of the bow, bowstrings, and arrows.

Klann, Margaret L. *Target Archery.* Addison-Wesley, 1970.
A guide for the improvement of the amateur archer's skills.

Pszczola, Lorraine. *Archery.* 2d ed. Saunders, 1976.
One of the Physical Activities series designed for high school use, this covers technique, safety, skill improvement, and equipment, with emphasis on various competition situations, rules, and team events.

Reichart, Natalie, and Keasey, Gilman. *Archery.* 3d ed. Ronald Press, 1961.
A complete guide to the techniques and fundamentals of archery.

Richardson, M.E. *Archery.* McKay, 1975.
A teach-yourself book.

Roberts, Daniel. *Archery for All.* Drake, 1976.
A guide to equipment, shooting, tournaments, and clubs in England. The chapter on shooting will be most valuable to readers in the United States.

Roth, Bernard. *The Complete Beginner's Guide to Archery.* Doubleday, 1976.
An illustrated introduction to the sport with practical advice on improving your skills, plus recommendations on the proper equipment, target practice, hunting and fishing, and participation in competition. An archer's information directory is appended.

Sullivan, George. *Better Archery for Boys and Girls.* Dodd, Mead, 1970.
A complete, enthusiastically written guide for younger readers, with good illustrations.

Other Materials

Archer's Handbook, National Archery Association.
Frequently revised and updated. Brief history, layout of various ranges, rules, and regulations for competitive archery, including national, international, and Olympic events. Suggestions for starting a club, selection of equipment by the beginner, and fundamentals of shooting technique.

Carter, Joel W. *How to Make Athletic Equipment,* Ronald Press, 1960.
Clear instructions for the crafting of arm guards, finger tabs, arrow curtains and rack, bow racks, equipment carts, ground quiver, target base and cover, as well as various bows and arrows.

Constitution and Bylaws of the National Field Archery Association.
Rules and regulations of the NFAA, games and shooting rules.

"What is Field Archery," a pamphlet prepared by: National Field Archery Association, R. D. 2, Box 514, Redlands, CA 92373.

Acknowledgments

The Boy Scouts of America is grateful to John W. Smith, Director, Olympic Youth Archery Program, Easton Sports Development Corporation, for his assistance in preparing this revised edition of the *Archery* merit badge pamphlet. The Boy Scouts of America is also grateful to the following individuals for their assistance in preparing other material used in this pamphlet: Richard A. Bryant, NAA certified instructor; Jim Dougherty, Ben Pearson Company, Zebco Division, Brunswick Corporation; Jack Rogers; and Ervin G. Kreischer, past president, National Field Archery Association of the United States.

Illustrations by Sandy Owens—pages, 7, 8, 10, 11, 13, 15–19, 29–36.